For Jesse, for making me feel this way

DOWN

SARAH DOWLING

Coach House Books // Toronto, Ontario

Published with the generous assistance of the Canada Council for the Arts and the Ontario Arts Council. Coach House Books also acknowledges the support of the Government of Canada through the Canada Book Fund.

LIBRARY AND ARCHIVES CANADA CATALOGUING IN PUBLICATION

Dowling, Sarah, 1982-, author
        Down / Sarah Dowling.

Poems.
Issued in print and electronic formats.
ISBN 978-1-55245-298-1. (pbk).

        I. Title.

PS8607.O9875D69 2014   C811'.6   C2014-904550-6

Also available as an ebook: ISBN 978 1 77056 395 7.

Purchase of the print version of this book entitles you to a free digital copy. To claim your ebook of this title, please email sales@chbooks.com with proof of purchase or visit chbooks.com/digital. (Coach House Books reserves the right to terminate the free download offer at any time.)

EVERYBODY LOOKS ALIKE
AND ACTS ALIKE,
AND WE'RE GETTING MORE
AND MORE THAT WAY.

I'VE GOT TO TELL YOU

I'm talking Cause I really
can't tell me are you grey
Say Cause I really Tell me
I'm not
If I can't tell I hope I'm talking
listen Cause I really need Tell me are you

really Tell me are you lonely
I'm not And Is it wet, Is it Cause
If I If I
can't tell you're real I hope that we'll Oh
Boy see I shouldn't let you but
Won't you If you tell you know
Cause I really Tell me are

you that somebody Cause I'm
not but just Say yes You
can't tell me Are you
talking you shouldn't but if I
if I let you go We talk
But don't know see if I promise you then

Can you

I've got yes. I've got this. I've got anxious. I've got serenity. I've got our existence. Of course disarray never included us. I've got sunshine. I've got an occupying attention. I may refer to, must inherently. I've got any. I've got any compulsive relationship, Sunshine.

Sunshine on a cloudy day, on a method. On expressed or implied. Not a thing or a person. On a cloudy day it will never be morning. On it. Cloudy in the way that we do this. Cloudy day talking, better for us. I've got one sexual method, described by forms of histories, of aesthetics.

When made present. When it's by the explicit. When it's cold, that relentless energy outside their excesses of sex. Outside their lives. It's cold outside and when it's linked. When it's the trembling cold outside the world.

I've got the month. I may by relentless excesses present the explicit. I've got their lives of us. The month of method and talking. The month of this it. Of course their energy would. The month it were day. I must refer. I've got disarray. May inherently. I've got the month to do a thing described.

I guess, or person. I guess sex. I guess an expressed or implied relationship. You'd say very compulsive. I guess histories. I guess any form of sexless method. You'd say not occupying I guess attention. You'd say that never included us.

What could make this aesthetics. What could make me feel that. Make me many. Make me better. What could make me sexless and sexual. Make me feel we. Make me feel made. Make me feel us. Make me feel matter. Make me feel this, for one. What could make me feel this commotion, this relationship to energy. What could make me feel this way.

I've got so much occupying. I've got a thing or person. I've got so much inherently. Not histories, never expressed or implied. I've got relentless. Honey, in the way. So much that an attention to forms. I've got so much disarray. I've got so much talking. I've got so much excesses. Honey included many of us. Honey, of course I've got that. I've got compulsive, got so much sexual.

The bees envy us. The bees of any sex. The bees of any means. The bees of any method. One made a matter of their lives. May, for us and for envy. Method and present. We do this better. The bees, sexless. It was Monday night. The bees, aesthetics, me.

I've got described. I've got the explicit. I've got the same state of trepidation. A sweeter song might be suffering, described by their energy. I've got a relationship. A sweeter song must refer, occupying anything. A sweeter person or sex, inherently that us. Sweeter, it pleases me. I've got all the forms of not.

Sweeter than the histories, than this relentless sexual aesthetics. Than never. The birds included to matter. The birds, a one, many of us. Expressed or implied excesses. The birds talking. The way that an attention may present the trees by disarray. In the trees, any method, the birds. In the trees, we do.

Well, I guess very compulsive. I guess for us. Well, I guess and for their explicit lives. I guess the method. Well, I guess and I, sexless. You'd say sexless, of course. You'd say nevertheless I guess we are part of this disorientation.

What could make me feel made. What could make me better. What could make disarray. This way, forms. This way of may not, never. This way of a relationship. What could make me feel we, that us. Very occupying method, attention. What could make me feel anything. This way or any person. What could make this a matter. Feel this one. Feel this expressed. Feel in the way of that attention. Feel this included, talking to us of it.

I don't need or implied. I don't need histories of excesses. I don't need no explicit lives. And for sex, of course, I don't need us. I don't need any present. I don't need no money and any compulsive energy. Money described by their relentless method. I don't need no aesthetics. I don't need no, inherently money.

Fortune or refer. Fortune or a sexual I. Fortune or it strikes eleven. Fortune or their. Fortune or sexless, this sexless many. Fortune or a certain pace and rhythm. Fortune to this stabbing pulsebeat. Fortune or a relationship to a sexual better. Fortune or fame occupying that method made us.

I've got by. I've got all the forms of matter. I've got all implied. Baby, that one included sex for us. I've got all the riches and for any person or thing. Not in the way of attention to excesses. I've got all it was ten o'clock. I've got their very method. I've got all the disarray. Baby, we refer.

One man can claim the explicit talking. One man can claim aesthetics. One man, never a course of expressed histories. Claim lives of this sexless it, I, us. One man described by many. One man must. One man can, may present one man, relentless and compulsive. One man can claim energy. One man can do any, inherently sexless.

Well, I guess each critical approach. Well, I guess to the kind of contact. Well, existing, I guess between people. Between peoples. I guess refer. I guess a relationship included sex. I guess this described an occupying method. You'd say sexual. You'd say forms made compulsive. I guess you'd say better that any person may I guess present their histories.

What can make this matter. What can make me feel us. Make me feel this method. What can make attention to excesses. What can make explicit disarray. What can make a relentless course we must do. Make me feel the very aesthetics expressed or implied. What can make me feel this in their lives of talking. This way that one inherently I, or thing. This way, not sexless, never sexless. Would that it were. This of us, by many. Make me feel this and any energy, for us and for it.

I THINK EVERYBODY
SHOULD BE A MACHINE.

I'VE GOT TO TELL YOU

Can you Can you Can you Can
I promise you If we talk and you know
But see
I don't know if I
shouldn't tell but if
I let you   can't I'm talking Are you
I'm not lonely just   Say yes

or say no Cause I really Tell me are
you wet Oh
Boy Won't you If you tell you know
that I shouldn't let you but
If I   can't tell   I hope
I'm not Is it Is it Cause I really
Tell me are you that

somebody listen Cause I really Tell me are
you can't
tell I'm talking if that's
difficult I hope I'm not
lost just Say Is it Cause I really Tell me are you that
somebody Cause I really You can't

tell I'm talking further

EVERYONE SLEEP

Sometimes I'm the sentimental songs I enjoyed when I was
a teenager liking youLike the buses glow like clouds and I
am a lonely hawk in a skyThat flies andYou were my hold
you in my heart with a very real prey (my prey) sat there
and told my friend how I felt

Right now I'm the ones I played when I experienced a girlFor the first time liking things is like a promiseIf there is a place further fromThen we'll keep it dry the maroon robe you know that one of these days (days) were numerous and today I sat there and told my friend how I felt

Sometimes I'm the first time I realized they were written in a language of snow goneUp from their calling I did not yet speak because you do the same thing every timeWe were in the place further from me I beg you do not goBut see tears (tears) that sat there and told my friend how I felt

Right now I realized too quickly that I think I've been holding backThis yes again being all over the time you do mornings in my heart with a very secret place (place) further from me I beg youProbably shouldn't tell you how I've got to tell you always how I sat there and told my friend how I felt

Sometimes I imagined being thrown from a plane over my prey (prey) likeIt's because you pick me up at the parking lot was crowded with a language I did not yet speak and I stood up right nowUp the block while everyOne of these days when you are alone I sat there and told my friend how I felt

Right now I'm not on a plane though and for days (days) everything was waiting againWith lunch in my mouth the tea I'll be coldIf you tell the world I've got to tell you the buses glow and further from this hawk was in a sky I did not yet see but sat there and told my friend how I felt

Sometimes I was in the same car over and over and liking sleep you knowOh that nothing can see tears that seem to prey (prey) that think yesAgain being all over everybody although I never weep I'm trusting youWith mornings in a sky a place further from me if I let this if I tell you I beg you do not go talking and telling my friendIt's you

I THINK EVERYBODY
SHOULD LIKE EVERYBODY.

BURY IT

m-hm
bury it

and then you're not even
sure I // I think if

well
well

If something // something is either
the burial is gonna have to be //
m-hm
gonna be safe

or maybe even // maybe you can
but it doesn't seem
possible m-hm

Well,
I really // I really
don't know

BRUSH

playing away against Sunshine
travel
) –
   found under a bridge
burns   a large house fire in the
beaches and   water   and

Hawks,   games will

    rend   with a team

Metals   . (

last   .

.   crews race   to

   coast

they're travelling, and the Sun

burns in a large house fire
properties   burning in the Sunshine
                state, with critical shortages
five runs weren't enough

            to bring people into
Metal,   . (   ) has
.   crews   to
. The fire
towns of   water and
Hawks   taking the lead

grave under a bridge   ,   the   Coast
        the house fire, this time
to enable water
            forty-five against
honey

, in March

    A single storey

, and another

Hawks on the week   and

      Travel

grass fire   the

water that   vast, sodden

                      clash against

            offering

        report on '

. Two sheds and some fences
        into   ravines
Hawks   abandoned
Travel, based

                            . —
            of the   Coast

and then you're not even
sure if it's
um if // if

it can probably be put in
reasonably // reasonable
for what

well
well

If something // something
You see but the only problem is
the burial m-hm

and you cannot
at least I don't think
I can or maybe
even // maybe

but it doesn't
Well I suppose it's

really // I really don't

STARLIGHT TOURS

before the found found found when found   were likely
his boy   in two   and cop caused
frozen   the an a more the forced guilty by
body
        frozen north industrial north   north   of handcuffs,
was   industrial   were industrial defend unlawful the
              area field,   area itself confinement judge
in in   with frozen   and found
   the marks   sentenced
     remote urban   *kneel*
field sprawl his were eight
           months
and wrists

        so to on on so

walk he walk   there

back, come back so-called   , were

sober and 'starlight and

                                        questions

    , kissed   ' clearly questions

settle   this

        , and isn't

he   asked

left. area

where

people

```
        but           his                        Yes, his
saw he says        friend had face as little cop
    , had              was        fresh soon friend
        had bloodied handcuffed blood as
friend, face   up. and on I
in to cut His bleeding his saw
the the    boy in    , him
backseat window his     was across there
and face full back his was
he
was blood. gash
yelling across


me
```

teenaged when   several
                                 one after how
who two   cases of several he
died more   of three men came
of men have men First were
                   driven who   found die
found intox
               froze people frozen in
frozen
            to to to such
           death a
   lonely
remote

a who who from of   it
cold   was where exposure   sprawls
winter taken screaming he on
night out   bitterly outskirts
                        bitterly   *kneel*
on him last cold on the
        seen nights river
cold   of cold and
winter   November

of   centre
the

, though a and him He who   The 'midnight on
    cold   in had was bitterly   , ride' bitterly
      winter was   fresh taken cold lonely cold
            bloodied field

                            out night night nights
drinking up.   on in and
      his a November dropped
night face night   , cold 1990 them
    when across winter off,
full   night
of
blood

had, though He the He but had had since
boy he says seventeen-   had   picked enough the
spending had   fresh him time had 'starlight
        had only blood his   ,   '
    drinking had one on   driven dump had
    the cut shoe his to him   become
time night had   face,   outside   public had
together he his across   knowledge
disappeared face his city and edge

yelling

a I I because
cop saw didn't said it
car ,
   , want no, was
pulled I open,
in friend, be more *kneel*
in front there know open
 the in than
me
  backseat
    that because just
and car I a
  with didn't scratch
was want
in to
the
back

YES.
IT'S LIKING THINGS.

BURY IT

and then
you're not even
sure if it's // um that
the place you bury it

it
can probably be
safe

for what? something //

something is either a half or three
quarters and
you cannot guarantee that
anything is gonna be

safe

at least I don't think
or maybe even // maybe
you can but it doesn't seem I

really // I really don't

BRUSH

best in this. close

operating once again under her WHITE area

glimpse through control *The best place* to take making

head in the wing also struggling (it has been

raining traffic through the South the South

port of — unveil. spearheading the terror's

structure like the rural direct opposition

hawks once again taking under her

kneel to both, and Rain

Central parts of raining for Corridor (

which is the linking   *parking lot on the*

right. The best place WHITE their new

's structure, 'exploring the —, the the

rural every two (in the Picture:

The present and lifeline *Walk into*

the woods, follow the northwest coast

there is a trail in the shape

a date for release their cornered and most

into the woods, follow prey and the next markets

, one township a weekend of rain a return to

the best place for development expected next year. Her

WHITE area. a sneak a *path near the pond.*

Go left, warms between your

links with rural this part of the coast

operating under her

adjoining grind reverted to set the

release *The best place* by list the spokes of the front

in such weak and to or. Prevailing sweep moisture

is rain. once again her WHITE *place*

soon more) WHITE) of WHITE shifting from

— the northwest front want. to set steel to turn *kneel*

near any of the dark bench areas, the heaviest

yes

hawks to the cutting

grounds allegedly *best* saying 'has been, is an

ideal hideout for the *kneel* of the rural comes

prey falls along the Coast drenched in the early *any*

of the dark during. told her More. In

and yes *The best place* earlier, the city's *The main trail*

its rural Dam and other popular Lower turn

over. Here. made the making The act

BURY IT

m-hm

you're not even
sure

the place you bury it
I // I think
well
well

we just heard that
You see but the only problem is
m-hm

and you cannot //
at least I don't think
maybe even // maybe
but it doesn't seem

m-hm Well
I suppose
it's a problem I

really //
I really don't know

YES, BECAUSE YOU
DO THE SAME THING
EVERY TIME.

I'VE GOT TO

Cause I really   can't
Say   is it   Cause I really Tell me
I'm not
I hope
listen Cause I really   Tell me are you

really Tell me are you Won't you And
if I'm not   wet,
If I If I   can't tell
          Oh

                    Tell me

are you empty I'm not just Say

yes
Can you Can you   Can you

Can I boy under you honey

m-hm

Can you tell everyone I should brush against this maroon starlight and save the robe Can I bury the songs and the morning the grey sunshine the fire and what I sometimes prey and what you right now

m-hm

how I honey

m-hm

honey sometimes I think you're getting further from liking
this from the buses from the cold

                                                    hm

from the plane the hawk the parking lot and the numerous
stars honey am I safe sometimes now and way under anxious
am I clearly honey the songs you honey honey

                                        m-hm m-hm

Can I bury the grey sunshine honey the grassfire the prey the hawk under snow Can you know where the robe is where's the tea in my mouth how honey

m-hm

Can you tell everyone Can I bury under safe Can you can you brush it clear over me sometimes honey

m-hm m-hm

Can you know how honey

m-hm

I've got to tell you sunshine got to tell everyone I think we should sing all the sentimental songs and tell the starlight bury way under morning and sunshine I've got to tell you to get everyone

m-hm

I've got to tell you to tell everyone I always think in my mouth I've got to get you and glow like the parking lot the snow the grey mornings the only passenger

Can I see you brush the car in the sunshine got to tell you
Can you robe the songs clearly tell me Can you bury me
honey Can I boy under you honey tell me

                                        m-hm

Can I think you're safe to hawk the starlight and brush
morning Can you beg the cold lunch the anxious prey
honey Can I brush over you liking things I think in the
place further from this tell me

                                        m-hm m-hm

honey

                                        m-hm

YOU DO IT OVER
AND OVER AGAIN.

I'VE GOT   YOU

    Can you   Can you
            promise   If I   and you know

    you shouldn't   but
    I let you
        I'm not lonely just

     say no Cause I really   are
  you   Oh   If

                         ,

  If   If

       tell me are you   Won't you

  listen Cause I really Tell me are you
  If
        if

  If

Number one is mornings
Number two is my coast
Number three is my sunshine
Number four is my feel

Number five is my girl
Number six is that somebody
Number seven is naughty
Number eight is my girl

Number nine is my mouth
Number ten is grey
Number eleven is my feel
Number twelve   or tea

Number thirteen is that somebody
Number fourteen is noiseless
Number fifteen is hot enough
Number sixteen   tell nobody

Number seventeen is my cigarette
Number eighteen   or robe
Number nineteen is my feel
Number twenty is soft soap

Number twenty-one is my chills
Number twenty-two is my hawk
Number twenty-three is my feel
Number twenty-four is small talk

Number twenty-five is my lonely
Number twenty-six is my girl
Number twenty-seven is my only
Number twenty-eight is my girl

Number twenty-nine is my feel
Number thirty is my coast
Number thirty-one is this real
Number thirty-two   or snow

Number thirty-three is my one
Number thirty-four is nobody
Number thirty-five   or dock
Number thirty-six is naughty

Number thirty-seven is my buses
Number thirty-eight is proud
Number thirty-nine is my girl
Number forty is my clouds

Number forty-one is my girl
Number forty-two   that's good
Number forty-three is my girl
Number forty-four   or flutes

Number forty-five is my feel
Number forty-six is my beach
Number forty-seven is my girl
Number forty-eight is bees

Number forty-nine is nobody
Number fifty is my coast
Number fifty-one is my sand
Number fifty-two   at most

Number fifty-three is that somebody
Number fifty-four is my tears
Number fifty-five is my girl
Number fifty-six is my feels

Number fifty-seven is my heart
Number fifty-eight is my keys
Number fifty-nine is my girl
Number sixty   or trees

Number sixty-one is naughty
Number sixty-two is my birds
Number sixty-three is baby
Number sixty-four   or words

Number sixty-five is my parking lot
Number sixty-six is my feel
Number sixty-seven is my hawk
Number sixty-eight is real

Number sixty-nine is my coast
Number seventy   or keys
Number seventy-one is dry toast
Number seventy-two is all these

Number seventy-three is my feel
Number seventy-four is my girl
Number seventy-five is a meal
Number seventy-six is my girl

Number seventy-seven is relief
Number seventy-eight is my stars
Number seventy-nine is naughty
Number eighty is my car

Number eighty-one is that somebody
Number eighty-two is my snow
Number eighty-three is my girl
Number eighty-four is the most

Number eighty-five is daily
Number eighty-six is my girl
Number eighty-seven is baby
Number eighty-eight   or kneel

Number eighty-nine is my girl
Number ninety is my card
Number ninety-one is that somebody
Number ninety-two is warm

Number ninety-three is nobody
Number ninety-four is nothing
Number ninety-five is prosody
Number ninety-six is music

Number ninety-seven is my whole
Number ninety-eight is my girl
Number ninety-nine is that somebody
Number one hundred is control

Number one hundred and one is my hawks
Number one hundred and two is my cross
Number one hundred and three is my girl
Number one hundred and four is my girl

Number one hundred and five is north
Number one hundred and six is my pass
Number one hundred and seven is my girl
Number one hundred and eight   or path

Number one hundred and nine tell nobody
Number one hundred and ten   flies
Number one hundred and eleven is my girl
Number one hundred and twelve is dry

Number one hundred and thirteen is my place
Number one hundred and fourteen is my girl
Number one hundred and fifteen is my sunshine
Number one hundred and sixteen is further

Number one hundred and seventeen is mornings
Number one hundred and eighteen is my feel
Number one hundred and nineteen is my coast
Number one hundred and twenty is this wheel

Number one hundred and twenty-one is my girl.

I've been working on *DOWN* since 2009. It began as different project, *Hinterland B*. For years, I was writing about a big, bare field. There was a body in it. The newspapers said that someone was gone. The newspapers said that someone had been found. These were not the same person. The TV kept on chattering, people lost interest, the cycle moved on. I was thinking about this field as secondary: not Hinterland A, but Hinterland B.

I thought that the hinterlands were the most rural and remote places. Turns out, this is not true. A hinterland is more familiar; the waste fields around ports and airports are hinterlands. A hinterland serves as a buffer between sanctioned spaces for living and working and the trade hubs where we are not supposed to go. They are the regions between the everyday and the truly rural lands that we too often imagine as depopulated.

I was thinking about what takes place in these areas: illicit sex, beatings, illegal dumping, kids forging their own selves and places. I was thinking about hinterlands as locations of secret pleasure and concealed terror. Invisible, off to the side, that hard, uncultivated and often contaminated ground seemed to hold the possibility for a strange coalition. I wondered what connections might be made in these discarded spaces.

At the same time that I was working on *Hinterland B*, I was also working on performance writing using song lyrics. I liked how the repetitions structuring chorus and verse shifted when stripped of their melodic accompaniment. Gertrude Stein said she was inclined to believe that there is no such thing as repetition, only insistence. Frank O'Hara said that what was happening to him went into his poems. This was insistence but with more anxiety.

This was happening to me. I was interested in the ways the lines became so tense and upset. I was interested in the ways they set off funny little moments of recognition.

It was hard to learn how to use these kinds of words: *tell me you want me*; *tell me you need me*; *tell me I'm into something good*; *tell me what you want to hear*; *tell me baby*; *tell me you love me*; *tell me why*. I was trying to write a text caught between being completely poignant and completely flattened. I wanted to write in the language of pop songs, a language for love and one that I did not yet speak. I wanted a text whose insistent and repetitive borrowing would not slide into critical superiority. I wanted to do it like a song does: over and over again. Machine-like but utterly sincere.

To my surprise, I saw that the words in these two projects over-lapped: the same hawks flew across the pages. Everything came back to the birds and the bees. It was all the tension between telling and not telling. I put the two together. In this way, *DOWN* became a book about likeness. Andy Warhol said that everybody looks alike and acts alike, and we're getting more and more that way. Maybe that's true. But I wanted to put this likeness in tension with the things that aren't liked, the things relegated to the hard-packed field. There is a kind of wager here: can we take this junk language and make the connection, flatten it all the way till we're living in the same environment?

If we look at the field, then we already are. So let's get there.

Major sources for the poems in this book include G. R. Swenson's 1963 *ARTnews* interview with Andy Warhol; Aaliyah's 'Are You That Somebody?' (1998, covered by the Gossip in 2010); the Temptations' 'My Girl' (1964, filtered through the 1991 film *My*

Girl, starring Anna Chlumsky and Macaulay Culkin); Frank Ocean's coming-out letter (2012); and Frank O'Hara's 'Morning' (1951). The 'Bury It' poems rework a brief conversation included in an otherwise-unrelated academic article about rhetoric; 'Starlight Tours' draws upon news reports on the initial investigation into the death of Neil Stonechild (1973–1990); the 'Brush' poems draw upon a variety of news sources and on text accompanying the photographs in Chad States's *Cruising* (2012).

OOOH, YOU MAKE ME LIVE

For many exchanges of manuscripts and ideas I am grateful to Rachel Zolf, Divya Victor, Julia Bloch, Janet Neigh, Maxe Crandall, Diana Cage, Gregory Laynor, Laura Neuman, Matt Goldmark, CAConrad, Jordan Scott, Jason Zuzga, Jena Osman, Megan Milks, Amaranth Borsuk and Jeanne Heuving. I'm grateful to Emma Stapely for giving me the text from which the 'Bury It' poems were made and to Dan Schank for introducing me to the work of Chad States, which has been so helpful. To my colleagues and students at UWB and at UPenn, thank you for our conversations.

Thanks to Susan Holbrook for your generous and sympathetic editing, to Alana Wilcox, Evan Munday, Leigh Nash, Stan Bevington, Sarah Smith-Eivemark, Heidi Waechtler, Rick/Simon and everybody at Coach House for your support of this project and your enthusiasm about my work. I'm especially indebted to Katrina Ohstrom for the beautiful cover photo, which was taken at Northeast/Edison/Julia de Burgos High in Philadelphia, a public school that was abandoned in 2002 and will soon become a Save-a-Lot supermarket.

Many thanks to the editors of the following publications, where excerpts of this book have appeared: *Harriet: The Blog*, *Line*, *Revista Laboratorio*, TrollThread, *The Windsor Review*, *Matrix*, *I'll Drown My Book: Conceptual Writing by Women* and *P-Queue*.

But most of all, thanks to Jesse Long for making it possible and making it good, to the pets for getting in the way, and to my friends and family for the broader context. Things mostly work and sometimes don't. It's such a relief to be with you all.

SARAH DOWLING is the author of *Security Posture* and *Birds & Bees*. Her poetry was included in the anthology *I'll Drown My Book: Conceptual Writing by Women*, and she is international editor at Jacket2. Originally from Regina, Saskatchewan, she currently resides in Seattle and teaches at the University of Washington Bothell.

Typeset in Aragon and Aragon Sans, from Canada Type.

Printed at the old Coach House on bpNichol Lane in Toronto, Ontario, on Zephyr Antique Laid paper, which was manufactured, acid-free, in Saint-Jérôme, Quebec, from second-growth forests. This book was printed with vegetable-based ink on a 1965 Heidelberg KORD offset litho press. Its pages were folded on a Baumfolder, gathered by hand, bound on a Sulby Auto-Minabinda and trimmed on a Polar single-knife cutter.

Edited by Susan Holbrook
Designed by Heidi Waechtler
Cover photo by Katrina Ohstrom

Coach House Books
80 bpNichol Lane
Toronto ON M5S 3J4
Canada

416 979 2217
800 367 6360

mail@chbooks.com
www.chbooks.com